CA'

CATCH

PETER CARPENTER

Shoestring Press

Typeset and printed by Q3 Print Project Management Ltd, Loughborough, Leics
(01509) 213456

Published by Shoestring Press
19 Devonshire Avenue, Beeston, Nottingham, NG9 1BS
(0115) 925 1827
www.shoestringpress.co.uk

First published 2006
© Copyright: Peter Carpenter
The moral right of the author has been asserted.
ISBN-13: 978 1 904886 32 7
ISBN-10: 1 904886 32 9

Shoestring Press gratefully acknowledges financial assistance from Arts Council England

For Amanda, Zoë and Beatrice

and in memory of
my father

ACKNOWLEDGEMENTS

Acknowledgements are due to the editors of the following
publications in which some of these poems, or earlier versions
of them, first appeared:

*Agenda, Critical Survey, English, The Frogmore Papers, Magma,
Navis, The North, Notre Dame Review (US), Orbis, Other Poetry,
Poetry Ireland Review, The Rialto, The Slab, Smiths Knoll, Tears in
the Fence* and *the TLS.*

'Achill' features on the 'Poetry Daily' Website; 'Scan' is in *The Gift*
(Stride); 'Old Cannon Wharf' in *Poetry South East 2000*
(Frogmore Press); 'Little Girl Lost' and 'A Retreat' in Reactions3
(Pen&Inc); 'Undercurrent' in *Paging Doctor Jazz* (Shoestring);
'Harvest Moon' in *Catalogue 2000* (Worple Press). 'The Sun' first
appeared in *The Black-Out Book* (Arc 2002); versions of 'A
Retreat' and 'A Woman in the Sun' appeared in *No Age*
(Shoestring 2001) and *Choosing an England* (Worple 1997)
respectively.

I am especially grateful to the following for their advice and
encouragement: Alan Brownjohn, Kevin Jackson, Michael Laskey,
David Morley, Toby Newton, Peter and Ann Sansom, Clive
Wilmer and Anthony Wilson. Also, thanks to all in the English
Department at Tonbridge and those involved with the Writing
Programme at the University of Warwick and the Arvon
Foundation at Totleigh Barton.

CONTENTS

What is this same?
This is the tune of our catch, played by the picture of Nobody
Shakespeare

1+1=a window   children's riddle

OLD CANNON WHARF

Past castle walls, punts,
exhaust fumes, new Pizza joint
at the bridge, our wharf's

a Jackson Pollock
close up: competition for
space in the green range

and white flowerings
of blackberry bushes; ragwort
and the odd willow

hanging in there; oak
and sycamore nibbled-at
and dusted along

the edge of things; tags
of buddleia scrambling up
round unused moorings;

the first spits of rain
in sky becoming water,
skimmed by damselflies;

crushed *Embassy*
packets; pigeon-shit dimples
on dark-stained wooden

benches; and a glance
ahead finds the lone angler
waiting for a bite,
part of this cast flow, curved like
a Henry Moore, his detail
then realised in scrutiny.

DOWNS

These are my showers coming up
and over from Headley Heath

my kite-fliers
my tinnitus of remote-controlled planes

my fairways bounded by resistances
and thicknesses of rough

                      my piles of rope-pie
horse-shit, forked and smouldering

my gallops with their bronto-boned
wood-pole divides
                   my footpaths running
white in after-rain chalk-water

my ghost-races looping down the hill
round Tattenham Corner into nowhere
but the Mr. Whippy and a hut
for mouth-scalding teas

my distances —
                but I'm trailing over
the final furlong, carrying too much weight,
feeling the slope, the going, the cold

ACHILL

Sweeneys has a line in gravel
and sand, everything pretty much:

breezeblock essentials, vanloads
of speeding undesirables, a fire

of tyres, judging from that billowing
across the water and the bind

of sound from fellas texting
and missing calls. Then there's

the bar that never shuts, flying really
flying... And the front room lined

with candles, a solid swirl
of stairhead, the couple going down

to the beach heightened in buzz
by the 'Govan sheen'.
                                    The lilies

were already there, pouting along
by the path — we just cut them from

wild and found the vases. About
us no muttering of prayer, but

black-headed sheep tearing away
uncannily into the backdrop

of grey-slicked stone, skylarks
and water, bog cotton. Well after

the last taxi, the plastic bags of
peat, still flapping, miles off.

TOWARDS CAP GRIS NEZ

and after the tidy auberge
we come upon it, and travel,
the two of us again, into

what might be gravel
infill or snow, on past
distractions of water

towers, razor wire
and war memorials,
straight up into something

fine as love high in
the channel air. In its mist
the crawl of the long distance

swimmers all goggled
and larded up, dipping
and rising against the swell.

We tiptoe their shingle,
pinch ourselves, stumbling
across this new element.

HOMAGE TO JOHN SELL COTMAN

Wherries less solid
   than cumulus
about its business

and the everyday
   gestures of water.
Hands prizing open

the jaws of eels.
   You sense futility
in the great work

rumbling on under
   human affairs
massive as those

Dunwich bells
   on the bed
of the etching sea.

HONEYMOON: SOUTHWOLD BEACH 1990

The beach-huts that stretch off down into that flatness
towards Sizewell B should be all boarded up now,
made safe for winter — their guessed-at interiors
devoid of flip-flops and sandy thermos flasks.

It's mid-afternoon, mid-December, but it could be
dusk or mid-morning for all the clues we're given
by the background grind of tide on shingle,
the freakish light on tankers off Sole Bay.

We'll walk straight into it though, with identikit
Drizabones, thick gloves, kids' beenie hats
and sensible shoes. Our children aren't with us,
and we're not certain, in this any-hour mist,

but they might be out there, aiming to rendezvous
by the Walberswick ferry, waiting to be born.

BREDON

for Amanda

Field of spring cabbage. Rotation
crop, stubble poking through.
Malvern Hills visible in heat
shimmer. I've always said I want
to live round here, but it's not
an option. Right into the woods
and then climb into south south
westerly gale. Ancient. Stones
set for a fire. Sheep poo. Zoë
remembers the pub we went to
before she was born. Mushrooms.
Which way. Notice: walls are living
history. Linseed: a vivid blue. Cling
film, lubricants, bio-diesel: green
energy. Buzzard/hawk/kestrel
reddish tint, wings tilted over sheep
and slurry. Deciduous shedders
only just going and it's the end
of October. So many ways. That bore
of a farmer didn't listen, didn't
consider revising.

We're shadows, wobbly
verticals on the lip of a natural
amphitheatre. Fragments.

HARVEST MOON

The huge harvest moon
hanging there come twenty
to ten this warm August night
reminds me of when Zoë
was born: the drive home
up and over the hill on
the A21; and the surprise
of that bloodied white face.

SCAN

2: OB/ GYN 3RD TRI

count on
    money-spider fingers

        pearls that will be eyes

locate spine of lights
    defined by vibration

            egg-hills that flex

our new settlement
    lightning sketched

            plot a course now

        ~

one in a million
    charcoal on paper

        a Henry Moore

bedded down
    in the underground

    curled for warmth

in on yourself
    until the all-clear sounds

        and you come up for air

THE BABY

after Carver

the baby worth its weight in liquidisers
the baby running a protection racket from the womb
the baby with the luminous green clock face
the baby with its own supermarket trolley
the baby chucking up gruelly stuff down my back
surprise baby
the clammy handshake, goo-goo smile,
never-says-this-never-does-that-presidential-candidate baby
the baby enjoying a good poo on the carpet
the baby with its finger on the button
the baby covered in flies
the baby we stare at but don't help
the baby that never cries
techno baby
the baby addicted to ketchup and raspberries
the baby with footballer's legs
the baby whose first word is 'jam-jar'
clever baby
the baby with ancient balding dreams
the baby that didn't show
the baby we never talk about
the baby at the centre of the universe

our baby

SEA STONES

Freshwater East, Barafundle, Broadhaven.
Re-remembered place-names glisten again,
sea-wet, sea-darkened, smooth as bone
in our open palms – tongues of sandstone,
wafers of lime, skimmers of slate, veterans
that we hold as tokens of our blessings, each
chosen from giving sand, clinging marram,
or, after close inspection, the compact
of elders in tide-pools. Entirely free.
I think to hoard them, still, at my age,
a romantic, but Zoë, my daughter, aged three,
already the conservationist, puts them in
her plastic bucket, and places them back,
as close as possible to where they had been.

AWAY

water you left
the tulips in

now pure
halitosis

sitting-room
Orwellian

wisteria going
crazy out the front

CATCH

We braved the swell with our catch
and slithered it into ice and salt.

'Pigs!' we joked, rank, still all at sea.
'Rat,' my girl whispered through the big hug.

Then we worked our stubby knives
along fine-combed markers of bone.

MOVES

We did not rehearse.
Things we cannot name
were left with lunar

toe-nail clippings,
a talcumed blue-
bottle playing dead

ant on the bath mat,
a bag of pre-
decimal coins, mating

paper clips, things
like pasta between cooker
and unit. Again: check

electricity, read gas,
tick things off
a mental list. In the fuss

you: remember ? Later
you find a king's head
florin, fluffed, heavy

in a lining; spend good
time over socks, patterns
you simply can't match.

COMING UP

Stuck in a tailback up the old A10
(with waiting-room benches at Liverpool Street,
those essays I wrote on Wordsworth and Keats,
smoke from the stubble past Audley End,

the first supervision, that Old Norse freak,
the pregnancy scare, the Dylan bore,
the gown and the scarf I hardly wore,
'relationships' formed during Freshers' week,

the girl from New Hall with mad, frizzy hair
who showed her first novel to Germaine Greer,
the Backs, the U.L., porters, the beer,
Leavis's death, the structuralist affair)

are memories of Addenbrookes seen from the train,
a tower wisping smoke, the unannounced rain.

LITTLE GIRL LOST

A nationwide search for the little girl lost.
Do you know this face? Can you picture
the bathtime routine? Please come forward.
Call this number in the incident room.
Cast your mind back. We have her toys displayed.
Eliminate these people in the reconstruction.

Answer me, answer me. Are you an echo?

Through a mist forming around dawn in the valley,
thanks to you out there, she's been found.
You heard her calling, climbed the rough line
of stone steps to the locked pavilion, saw her
huddled shape, rang this number. Dawn, alone,
out walking your labrador. Please come forward.

Answer me. Are you an echo? Are you an echo?

A nationwide search. The incident room.
She's been found. Thanks to you out there.
You climbed the steps, looked in at her shape.
You might be a hero, claim your reward.
You pictured the routine, knew the face.
Eliminate all the others from our enquiries.

Are you an echo? Are you an echo? Answer me.

WORKSHOP

for Ann Sansom and Anthony Wilson

1. Begin writing. Two minutes, without stopping, anything that comes into your head.
2. Locate obligatory maniac in group. Write, without stopping, about maniac.
3. Show religious tolerance when deaf Methodist tells rest of group very loudly that he 'doesn't think that any of this is really poetry'. Fix grin, move on, file away for future reference.
4. Steal things which stick in your head like 'spit-grilled fish' or a 'well-laid table of fields'.
5. Catch breath at dawn workshops of sun and shadow. See faces in the wood.
6. Wonder at two a.m. moths cuffing exposed lights. Drink a tad more house white.
7. Contribute to anthology of faces, hands, gestures. Sense life-histories easing themselves free.
8. Miss them/it. Fail to erase maniac from memory banks.
9. Remember the session on doors. Visualise one. Write down the word 'door'. Leave until it opens out into something.
10. Underline any of the above if it rings true.

Begin writing again for two minutes, without stopping, yes, by yourself this time.

The first thing that comes into your head. Don't analyse, don't get all defensive.

Don't stop.

There.

Anyone like to read theirs out ?

THE LESSON

Third up. You've had all your
lessons with Mister Fennimore
after class, have done it anyway,
swimmingly, twice before. Back there
at Morden Farm, of course

it is. In line, fudged self somewhere
down there in polish that smells of sick,
your passage has that thing about
the earth being 'stippled'... *According
to St. Mark* and it's your turn now

and for all you're worth you go for it,
through frost-glassed door as brisk
as anything along pee-green corridors
out into the yard, voices still playing
tricks, after-reaches of 'kiss chase'

there all the miles home, although,
just for a flicker, you take in hessian
thrown over the kerb into the road
for the blood. Accident, another gone,
you think, that'll flipping teach you.

SLIP CRADLE

Wooden palm
cupped to catch
each sharp chance of air.

Avocado stone once
giant in its slats
routinely taken
by some long-dead slipper.

Vertical against
the back of a pavilion,
it's as emphatic as a
beergut over a belt.

*Watch it all the way
into your hands.*
So went the advice. And
Keep your head absolutely still.

Moss seams stitch its feet.

Just thinking about it
makes my fingers hurt.

THIS SPORTING LIFE

                                then
flying winger or
full back on the overlap
midfield dynamo

keepie-uppie challenger
to Dario Gradi
(left right thigh head knee)

sprinting, harrying,
making it from box to box,
showing for the ball

                                now

strawberry flush, heart
murmur, huge sweat, fatal
hesitation on the ball,

staking out the centre
circle, nutmegged, done for
pace, sweeping behind

the back four, osteo-
arthritic big toe,
genuinely, agonisingly

                                slow

LOOT

You want me to help clear the loft.
I break into the enclosure of air
and peer up: torchlight trickles
feebly across a lagged tank,

sheeted shapes of stuff deemed
too precious to chuck: Subbuteo
teams with their long-handled
keepers; infantry, WW2,

hand-painted for the Russian Front.
The temperature drops a couple of degrees.
Your running commentary ensues.
'Maybe your two would like these ?'

Or 'Shall we keep that, Pete ?'
at grand-dad's Masonic robes
(purple, sheathed in cellophane), complete
with spooky initiation rules.

'He was a good man — loving he was.'
Enough here for two or three trips
to the tip. Hours in, I hand down
a bag ridged with florins and half crowns.

I know their feel. They'd lived for years
on the ledge in my parents' bedroom
stacked into tiny chimneys or towers.
Once or twice I snuck in before

the dawn chorus to pocket some.
The blanketed bodies didn't stir bar
their respective breaths being taken.
I don't imagine either of them even noticed.

The remaining apple-trees are bowed, crusted with moss. One has a wooden crutch to prevent its trunk from bellying out on the grass. The quality of the lawn is poor. Again, moss, patches of scarified earth, unevenness. Two bird baths, pine-green, both made in mother's pottery days, glazed and etched into, with simple and striking images of skeletal birds. Egyptian in profile. The area is unpeopled.

Round one side of the house, where the walnut tree stood (before the storm) is a coal-bunker, cat's tongue pink but mottled green through years of damp. A couple of crows, mid-morning, stake out their territory. They spear offerings of crusts and stale cake ahead of starlings and pigeons. Squirrels display an ability to scavenge upside down in trees.

Diagonally opposite the back-door, under cover, where a vine still produces dusty, shrivelled grapes, was where father's exercise bike once lived. It's been removed. Part of the clearing process. Johnson took it. He skipped it. It was no bother — easy with the two of them.

UNDERCURRENT

I never get much further than the end
of track two, the second take of 'My Funny Valentine'
and it's usually played as a cheddar mash
is being prepared for chicken with that balsamic vinegar
and honey sauce or I'm chucking a salad together
capriccioso. The ancient beat-box atop the fridge
sometimes skims on or sticks but no matter
when it's you and me, my dear, the children just about in bed.

Those first six notes of Bill Evans' virtuoso piano
and Jim Hall's 'stop-and-go' guitar, as the sleeve-note
puts it, keep on coming as I try to blank out my mother,
following her stay of just a few days, poor love,
and my unwarranted annoyance, my bleak anger
at her eating habits — like a horse, double dose of meringue
or cake, trilled with, why not, cream or what-have-you, killer
for the stroke-victim and late-diagnosed diabetic — or her
'that's just like the first flat we had at Barnes together'
verdict on any house with veranda or the flicker
of her touch-paper hands a-twitch like caught fish
at the end of a line or right foot quivering over
phantom passenger-side brake as I overtake or indicate
to move into another lane on the A21 or the glaze
that comes over her face as we try to get real
about the future and the detail of her daily routine.

And this little duet has the right blend of 'wistful melancholy'
and 'rhythmic precision' to be given its own sleeve-notes,
I'm thinking, were anyone madly attentive enough
to precise delivery over the years, the muttered explosions
at nothing, the as-ever-unresolvable attrition
of fret and string, its extended intermodulation,
its staggering shifts in tempo and expression, until the machine
blips us forward into the alternate take of 'Romain'.

WASH AND SET

Sometimes, like now, an April three-fifteen,
with a class of twenty set still in a text,
I think of you in that 'what-might-have-been'
mode, oblivious to which shop is next

to which along the High Street, automatic
pilot clicking you on to buy another needless
wholemeal loaf, some skimmed milk, seedless
Australian grapes, nothing too dramatic —

enough to fill a basket, to allow an exchange
of eye contact, to give the day some shape.
Inheritance, probate, estate: all words strange
to you last year: some stray or escape

you utterly on the phone. Your hair could do
with a wash and set. There's the gas and water too.

II

HORTON

'Go before me, and show me all those dreadful places' (Dickens)

'jumped out the window – flipping crazy' (clapping song)

i

down an avenue
            make your way
as best you can
            dark on
the far side of town
along the slips
(dwelling near a ruined building)

lines of barred windows
    over the wall

our camps

(Help me Lord
    When I would
    Fail Thee)

in the fires at night

    Help me Lord

gather the stones

ii

whereas recognition
of the inherent dignity
and of the equal
and inalienable right

in the fires at night

    there are no rules

there's darkness

iii

    from 1947 'c' and 'd'
were also used on some
plot numbers suggesting
that the plot might now
    accommodate four bodies

    young woman
arranging her hair
(another rests on the bed)

Article 3: everyone
has the right to life
liberty and security
of person

*(when hope would surrender
   to dark dispaires)*

    advice: read
        nothing and make
for the sea

iv
                    that way barbarism
prevailed – down an avenue
dark nameless

beneath our feet

an underground
    London
a hidden
    Eden
from the Latin
    for garden

angels in the trees

                    right there

v

    in painting
there are no rules –

    young boy-poet
with asthma

(another in the padded cell)

    young woman
taking a siesta

(another removes chamber-pot)

inmates at the door

    lacuna

we arise and sing

vi

however according
to a memorandum
1 Feb 1932 from
Chief Office LCC

Mental Hospitals
to Farm Bailiff Horton
now inserted in
6336/1 the cemetery
was not consecrated

Domine Dirige Nos

vii

what is important in a man
is his individual share in
what is common to all men

what are we then

(Deposited by the Patients' Service Manager)

viii

the men had been trained
to read Shakespeare
and continued to do so

OmletOmlet dis is dein
Vater spook

zanezanezane

questionable shape

what are we then

(please re-instate commas to the original)

ix

the smell of the land
from the Latin
lost plots past plans
for garden cities

fresh-tarred pavements
soft in the head

paupers' graves

the cemetery is clearly shown
    on Sheet XIII,
4 Apr 1902 – 29 Mar 1955

the memory's still strong

    there's darkness

x

    visions
angels in the trees
    heads on fire

water-towers
(all those cold baths)

young women flying
    with a rope

jumped out the window
(she went thatta way)

railings
        tippers
the articles

                the lime

xi

ancient
   admissions

   bricks
to
   dust

(when night comes down
   and the stormes
are raging

fill my soul
   with the strength
of prayer)

scatter us
   lord
      to the four winds

III

PUBLIC WRITTEN DECLARATION

for Kevin Jackson

to set humour at humour's throat

to free art from the dead weight of the real world

to explore flux

to be a machine

to reconcile vertical-horizontal, male-female, heaven-earth

to have it all my own way as often as is humanly possible

to tell stories (I got sick and tired of the Purity!)

to make an intelligible area of the whole wall

to celebrate the blossoming of a new culture and a new civilisation

to get out a little more

to buy that Malborough *Cloudy Bay* bin-end from Majestic on my way home

to celebrate the strangling of the vulture

to celebrate

PROPHET

wants to address the queues
for the ranks of black cabs

those striding past the flower-stall
and the Late Prices Standards

outside Charing Cross,
and the harried folk driven, oh

so driven, short-stepping it down
towards the ticket-barriers

for escalators and already-jammed
platforms for District or Bakerloo,

wants to freeze frame them somehow
and say firmly, not losing his rag,

not wearing rags or a giant
grinning Blair mask, not three-parts-stoned,

not naked, not all sanctimonious
philanthropist, but in level tones,

knowing the pressures, with respect
to you and yours, wants to say,

quite simply, you're wrong,
there's nothing at the end of this,

you're not actually creating anything
(and cut the 'wealth creation' comeback)

and one day you might stop, sit on
a bench, study the paving and

the sparrows pecking round your feet,
and think where it's all taken you

THE SUN

Out where Austrian blinds open
onto a ribbon development
past new-insured rooftops
along the Godstone valley
you deliver yourself each dawn.

Father of total block,
delineator of rose and turd,
patroniser of asylum seekers,
slow there for the sleeping policeman,
caricature the foraging beggar !

Semtex-planter and blanket-bomber
of Docklands and Spaghetti Junction,
dogged graffiti artist, tagger of highrise
and semi, pledged laureate, pronounce
now upon the restoration of Windsor !

RED EYE

for Boris Mikhailov

There you go spoiling it all for us
the grand illusion the big gesture

or whatever. Will they show?
All red eye and scar tissue: scribbles in biro

on a dissertation officially passed,
skim read, filed, forgotten. A bare arse

or raw crack, a display of sores. Eczema:
a fire from deadwood: they're movie extras,

pure *Night of The Living Dead*, you know
that bit when they all freeze, come right up close,

clasp you in recognition. *We're back, it's us,*
old mate, old mucker. Snow blindness, a flash.

SUMMIT

i

jokers
    arms akimbo
put their baboon arses
into it
    close up the ripples
just gulls' wings
           the craft
fronted with pound signs

commerce
    sails set   regularity of hopes

one high little cloud

ii

is a deluge
an impassable route
    a signature
of observation

see there
        the squiggle of briar
snowed under
    to the right

iii

Austerity. The mad
antlering skates. Mouths opening
in cold. The dutiful

windmill down in the
horizon. Encampments,
a national flag, a bird

39

scratched above a ruin.
Suddenly you get it —
they're singing.

                  iv

masonry the ordinary
            dead heaped head to head
unaware of such a
            composition any statement
the message to be
            had in the orderliness
of shadow effects

                  v

       voluptuous
          creatures
          monstrous
          lobsters
            hare
          pheasant

       tiny flicker
       of life – a lizard

   far in the
          creases
          of land
          hunters

            a
          speck
          red
          under
          sky .

September 2001

SUCH KNOWLEDGE

Immersion in a world of velcroed pizza,
inflatable parrots, Idris the dragon
seeking sanctuary in Ivor's boiler, broken
only by Radio Four drift on the 'real' IRA,
Adams and some Unionist all aglow
over the latest on decommissioning,
analysis of compensation for culls in Devon
and Cumbria, a reminder that fifty-six years ago
to the day, thousands of feet below
a Superfortress, Hiroshima lay like a pretend city
in all its working detail, before a terrible togetherness
flashcarded new words and meanings its way.

A RETREAT

Orderly? — Christ, no. Charred leaves ring
shell-holes in the woods. Children
prised from their warm pits howl
and howl. Receding, over there,
what was ours. Family cars
gleam in the drives of two-storey,
red-tiled houses. Fruit trees blossom
in empty fields. We come away with our lives.

Hang on though, there's a kind of cheer,
a ripple of cat-calling applause from
the back of the column. Look. There
they are. Way below us, easy meat,
within range of the foremost enemy snipers
down in the land we held, seemingly
oblivious, a couple hanging on to each
other for dear life, necking like crazy, almost
motionless. They're already becoming

a dot, a myth, a joke. We listen out
for firing. Laugh them off. The idiots
who hugged themselves to death...
No, nothing. Come on. They're lost to us.

RETURNS

I'm pleased for my own sake that you didn't let on
about the dream that kept coming back to him
long years after the war
        when the runways up there
were all weed-cracked and the giant bombers had either gone
for scrap or were kept as tourist-traps in hangars.

        (You know — the one after the forced landing
with the undercarriage gone and the men
on fire who couldn't stop screaming.)

        It re-surfaced with Blair
and Bush on Iraq. Then that book on Dresden.

        The fire will return,
said the local bard, watching by the Elbe
as the great synagogue burned —
        it will make a long curve
and then come back to us.

VALEDICTION

Grey-green hills and then the city
    from the downs.
                    Rivers now long
    underground.
                    The Wandle. The Fleet.

Here is where we must say goodbye
and go with the night-wind driving
    across the deserted golf course.

Our hands shake
           miles apart.
                    We're out of here.

KILLER

i.m. Kenneth Curtis

Prefects in Carew whispered 'thumbscrews',
made you the 'killer' of repute for first-year ingenues.
The same man who threw us *Persuasion*,
interrogated Blake, spoke of the 'language of men',
gave me *Death of a Son* to read last lesson
in his rain-drummed hut. It was something else. Ken,
you know how words come, unbidden,
a quarter of a century on, how they can settle in

the right order. Wordsworthian negotiator
of fairway and rough! Pacer past chalk pit or
drought-fissure ! You understood life's grammar
of diminishing returns. It's close on five to four,
and you're striding for home, natural teacher,
up Hessle Grove, no bigger than this hand.

THALASSATHERAPY

Granville, 1917

We might imagine them filing in from the Place du Maréchal Foch
or Place du Plat Gousset before moving out via Point du Roc
to Cimetière Notre Dame. They start upright, in ranks,
under orders until they're off to exhibit masterpiece flesh

out past frond-scabbed rocks. But we'd be wrong.
None of them can move without another set of arms
to lift them into a chair. Fears are everyday: threats
of rain, youngsters crabbing, couples here

for a flutter at the casino, a chance to score.
In the ocean a square's marked off. They're lowered
into soft frond-forests, bobbing wigs. Limbs all milky
transparencies in the shallows. They sway. They dive

slo-mo into the bafflement of brine, swished by
rubbery knots. Unknowingly they pop olive blobs.
They have the indignity of not being dead: skin on
fast-forward, shrivelling apricot-style. At low-tide

a fresh no-man's land is exposed: toes can't tell
an urchin from a towel. Back inside, they gaze
unhealthily at post-card hopes. Each hand's
a distinctive sepia, an imagined room or face.

DIVERSIONS

A year on to the day
from your cremation
and the exit sign
from the M11 flashes
that the M25 is closed
at Junction Thirty.
Split second decision:
no toll at Dartford,
no Blackwall Tunnel,
'yes' to the one Sunday ferry
running out of Woolwich.

We share a baguette,
try to make it a bit
of an adventure: there,
the Thames Barrier; here,
the slop of ash-grey water
roughing up the cloud-cover
above and ahead of us.
We loop onto the A20.
To the east the fire
that's stalled everything
anti-clockwise back
to Junction Three.

For a week or so
uncountable specks
will fall steadily
on the rose-beds
of Travelodges
still able to offer
a special weekend rate.
Hardly a thought for
the steady progress
of your boxed-in body
rolling straight
into the flames that day.

THE TENTH

There — with the home nine to go.
A regulation par four ahead:
three wood, seven iron, two putt.

There — under the flight-path
of how many hopeful drives —
some topped, bobbling fifty yards or so,
others hooked onto the cinder and sand
of that newly-established bridleway —
a few though steepling for ages in the air,
the product of some momentary grace,
a reverent silence as they land,
running on and on down
that shudder of slopes
you negotiated so often.

This is where we leave you.

Each of us takes a turn
swirling out
those bits that were you.

We'll leave you
for golfing shoes
with baroque tongues
and screw-in spikes
to march you along
with the banter
and the tap-ins
to the eighteenth
down past disused chalk pits
to the clubhouse
you never frequented.

There —
the jar's empty.

We turn away
and make for the cars.

WOMAN IN THE SUN

Josephine Hopper, South Truro, 1965

'I'd sit up here for you way into
most afternoons. All you really wanted
was to get out, catch the sun,
miles from our little differences.

You were besotted. How you'd create!
I shed my skin like there was no tomorrow.
Another row, another flesh tone...
Then we'd smoke, lie on the bed,
read, play a hand or two
of poker. I'd put together a stew.

Hard to think we were ever that young,
ever that sure of how things were.
You kept my breasts firm for me,
I'll give you that. Your hands
speckled with age spots, waiting to be
classified, you old Galapagos creature.
Your brush flicked out its tongue.

Fall now. Any gas station or diner
an Eden of colour, form.
No need for any company.
Or over here, a white wall warm
with the image of me,
slung out on this recliner,
taking things in.'

IN HEAVEN

There'll be a really decent frying pan,
a store of light like it is here just past
nine thirty some immovable June evening,
and a frozen rapidice jacket thing
to chill another Sauvignon, fast.

COE FEN

for Clive Wilmer
on his 60th birthday

you point it out to me
this place
to graze the eye
note the levels —
here a shimmer
of springtime buds

downstream
a glaze of mist

and carved in stone
a martlet
stilled
for centuries
as this crest
on a college wall —

but shush now

from a lilac bush
badly in need
of cutting back
a robin
ups and leaves
for Coe Fen

then Lammas
and on to where
the rivers join
(Paradise
is it)

until it is truly
nothing

THE TREE

Christmas is a space for us
to believe in: it's a box-room
somewhere near the top of the house
all set up for unexpected guests.
Under the bed plastic bags wait
misshapen with wrapping paper
french sticks, crackers, trimble.
And through the double-knit dark

(when the time's right) a young girl
peeps in and gasps to herself
at the tree that's taken root
in the fawn carpet — its top growth
nudging the ceiling, sprouting baby
antlers, a regular miracle, for real.

NOTES

'Horton': the sequence's 'centre' is the Horton Cemetery off
Hook Road, Epsom where as many as 9,000 mental patients, war
casualties, soldiers and children lie unmarked in this burial site.
See Iain Sinclair's *London Orbital* (Penguin).

'Red Eye': the poem refers especially to the bomzhes, the
homeless, of Kharkov, featured in Mikhailov's *Case History*.

'The Sun' has a source in Baudelaire and 'Valediction' a source in
Pound.

'Summit': 'Venise, Le Pont Du Rialto' (Canaletto), 'Environs De
Harfleur, Neige' (Monet), 'Patinage pres de Dordrecht' (Jan Van
Goeyen), 'La Barricade, Rue De La Mortellerie, juin 1848' (Ernest
Meissouier), 'Nature Mort Aux Homards' (Delacroix): these five
paintings, all in the Louvre, are sources.

'Returns': the book referred to is Frederick Taylor's *Dresden*
(Bloomsbury).